M

THE
RIGHT
WAY

THE
RIGHT
WAY

Navigate the minefield of modern manners

Lauren McCutcheon
Introduction by A.J. Jacobs

D&C

David and Charles

First published in North America
by David & Charles
an imprint of F+W Publications, Inc.
4700 East Galbraith Road
Cincinnati, OH 45236
800-289-0963

Conceived and produced by
Elwin Street Limited
79 St John Street
London EC1M 4NR
www.elwinstreet.com

ISBN-13: 978-1-58297-465-1 paperback
ISBN-10: 1-58297-465-9 paperback

Printed in China

Cover design by David Wardle
Layout design by Maura Rosenthal
Illustrations by David Eaton

Contents

Introduction

By A.J. Jacobs, Editor-at-Large, Esquire magazine, and author of the bestseller *The Know-it-all: One Man's Humble Quest to Become the Smartest Person in the World*

I'm in a bit of a bind. You see, I was sent this exceedingly clever book called *The Right Way*. And it has changed my life.

Just this morning, thanks to this book, I sneezed the Right Way (into the crook of my elbow). I washed my hands the Right Way (including under the fingernails). And I am currently sitting at my desk the Right Way (computer screen directly at eye level).

The only problem? The book did not tell me the Right Way to write an introduction. So here I am, stuck trying to figure it out myself.

Perhaps I should focus my introduction on the impressive army of experts rounded up by author Lauren McCutcheon. You want to know the Right Way to make a cup of tea? This book doesn't offer advice from some shmo who has boiled a few pots of Orange Zinger for his in-laws. You get wisdom from the Grand Poobah of tea himself—namely, the Chairman of the United Kingdom Tea Council. You want to know how to eat ice-cream without spilling it on your pants? The official "Professor of Scoopology" at Ben & Jerry's provides the answer.

Or maybe I should try another tack. Maybe this introduction should take an historical view. I could babble a bit about ancient instruction books such as the *Compleat Angler* and *Art of War*, and make a case that *The Right Way* follows in their grand tradition, though with less war and fishing. And with more charming illustrations.

Or perhaps I should stress the peril that you face if you insist on ignoring this book. You will be consigned to living life the Wrong Way. When you greet someone, your hand will be like a flaccid trout. You will mow your lawn into a bunch of ugly, uneven patches. You will try to climb into a hammock and end up smacking your butt on the ground. I can't say for sure that you will die miserable and alone in a house with 14 cats and a ferret named after one of the Bronte sisters, but you get the idea.

Or maybe—here's a thought—there's no single Right Way to write an introduction to this book. Maybe it's one of the many gray areas in life. And let's face it: Gray areas are a pain. Which is why I'm delighted that the topics covered in *The Right Way* aren't gray. I've learned there is a Right Way to sharpen a pencil. And eat a cherry tomato. And dry out an umbrella. And doing these the Right Way will improve your life. So please read this book. Just not in a bathtub or a lake or a swimming pool (see page 14).

—*A.J. Jacobs*

BEGINNER LEVEL

- ✓ Load a Toilet Roll Holder
- ✓ Read a Book
- ✓ Sharpen a Pencil
- ✓ Wash Your Hands
- ✓ Eat an Ice-Cream Cone
- ✓ Sneeze
- ✓ Blow a Bubble with Bubblegum
- ✓ Squeeze a Tube of Toothpaste
- ✓ Open a Bottle of Champagne
- ✓ Get out of a Car
- ✓ Pose for a Camera
- ✓ Remove an Adhesive Bandage
- ✓ Tie a Shoelace
- ✓ Light a Fire
- ✓ Start a Mexican Wave
- ✓ Blow out a Candle

Load a Toilet Roll Holder

Expert advice from the British Hospitality Association

Toilet paper has a natural curve when sitting on a toilet roll holder. If you work with this natural curve, it can provide optimal sanitation and comfort during the most important of daily personal hygiene maneuvers. Below are examples of the elegant, efficient Over-Hung method (see Fig. 2); and as a warning to us all, the plain wrong Under-Hung method (see Fig. 1).

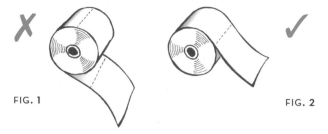

FIG. 1   FIG. 2

Note how two squares of paper are visible in Fig. 2, which allows you to quickly draw and liberate your bundle of toilet paper with one, smooth swipe of the arm.

The natural curve of the Over-Hung Method allows the roll to stand fast after a One-Handed Tear, but the Under-Hung Method creates a calamitous tendency for the entire roll to unravel (see Fig. 3). Executing the One-Handed Tear on an under-hung roll is a game of sanitary Russian roulette. You will lose—and there is no re-rolling the unwound toilet roll.

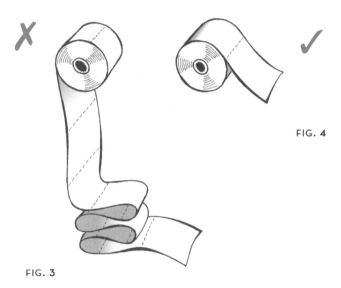

FIG. 4

FIG. 3

Read a Book

Expert advice from Nancy Pearl, author of *Book Lust* and the inspiration
and model for the Librarian Action Figure

The Right Way to read a book is less about reading style—reading the last page first is not exactly correct but is fairly benign—and more about physical respect. Bathtubs, swimming pools, and lakes are not places where you should read a book (see Fig. 1). A book is not a doorstop, booster seat, coaster, or makeshift desk.

FIG. 1

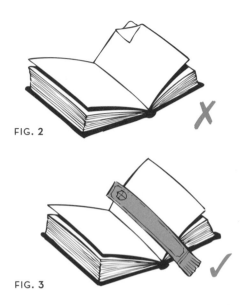

FIG. 2

FIG. 3

While it is perfectly permissible to mark up one's own book, it is wrong to alter the appearance of any book on loan from a library or a friend. One item essential to proper maintenance of bound pages is a bookmark (see Fig. 3). Portable and lightweight, this moveable signpost, which can be a designated bookmark or simply a clean scrap of material or paper, indicates the exact location of one's place between pages, thereby rescuing them from unsightly permanent creases that mar their delicate corners (see Fig. 2).

Sharpen a Pencil

Expert advice from Bob Imbs, Product Manager at Dixon Ticonderoga, maker of "The Best of its Kind" pencils

There is nothing quite as satisfying as a well-sharpened pencil—and nothing quite as frustrating as a dully tipped, fuzzy-marking pencil, a pencil with a ragged gripping surface, or a pencil lead that breaks upon impact. Fortunately, achieving a properly sharpened pencil is 10 percent method and 90 percent equipment.

First: The pencil. The Right Kind is fully bonded: Its leaden core is solidly sandwiched in a central groove. The Wrong Kind is glue-bonded: Its core is cheaply affixed with glue and breaks easily, exiting the pencil shaft bit by bit.

Second: The sharpener. Automatic-stop, electronic models; heavy-duty metal crankers; even inexpensive plastic sharpeners with new enough blades do the trick quite nicely, whittling down the wood to create a smooth, pike-like tip. Paring knives, razor blades, and other such apparatus should never be used to sharpen a pencil (see Fig. 1). Doing so results in an uneven, ungrippable wooden cone and lopsided leaden points that either break upon impact or create lifeless, imprecise gray lines.

Third: The sharpening. Choose a hole whose diameter is most equal to that of your pencil (see Fig. 2). Insert. Hold tightly and apply firm, light pressure while the wood whittles away. Extract stylus from device—and bathe in the satisfaction that yours is a perfectly-shaped writing implement.

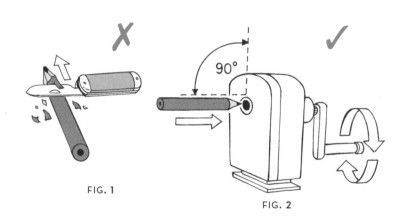

FIG. 1

90°

FIG. 2

Wash Your Hands

Expert advice from the U.S. Centers for
Disease Control and Prevention

Washing your hands is a personal choice. But it should be a personal priority. Not washing your hands after you go to the bathroom—apart from being a filthy habit—can have a serious effect on your health.

The Wrong Way to wash your hands is to perform the Quick Rinse (see Fig. 1). Whether the water is hot or cold, it is little more than wishful thinking to attempt to drown those sinister germs. They're dug in, waiting

FIG. 1

to rush you as soon as you place your hands near your mouth, nose, or eyes. A quick shake of the hands won't dislodge them, nor will it dry your hands. And wet handprints on your jeans are singularly unattractive.

The Right Way is not much more complicated or even more time-consuming than the Quick Rinse. When you wash your hands, use soap and warm, running water (see Fig. 2). Make sure you wash the fronts and backs of your hands, your fingers, wrists, and under your fingernails for at least 10 to 15 seconds. When drying, use a disposable towel and pat your skin, rather than rubbing, to avoid chapping and cracking.

FIG. 2

Eat an Ice-Cream Cone

Expert advice from Rachel Kamins,
Professor of Scoopology, Ben & Jerry's

Ice-cream, as scooped into and served from an edible cone, is a tricky treat. What reader does not recall such youthful calamities as delicious scoops sacrificed to gravity and fingers begrimed with uneaten chocolate, vanilla, or strawberry?

There is a Wrong Way to consume this hand-held dessert, and that is cone first. The brittle, upside-down birthday-hat-shaped pastry is tempting to crunch, particularly from the point. But one mustn't, as the cone's intactness is vital to the safe containment of the scoop it supports (see Fig. 2).

There is a Right Way to enjoy a cone of ice-cream, and it is scoop first (see Fig. 1). Top-down licks or nibbles must be carefully placed, with special care to errant drips as they descend. Begin biting the cone's upper-

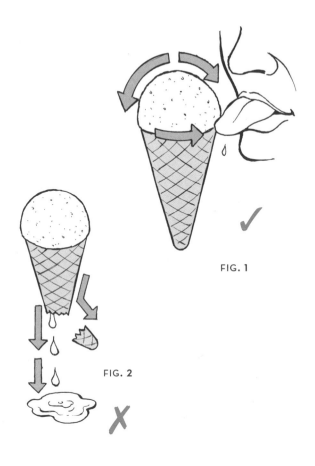

FIG. 1

FIG. 2

most edge when—and only when—the level of ice-cream has dipped below the crown of the cone. Eat an ice-cream cone with care, and relive none of childhood's wanton suffering.

Sneeze

Expert advice from Dr. Frederic F. Little, assistant professor of medicine, Boston University

Sneezing is a sudden-impact physical phenomenon with high-impact potential. Do it the Right Way and experience one of nature's most cathartic forms of relief. Do it the Wrong Way and demonstrate poor manners—and poorer hygiene.

Figure 1 depicts a commonplace but nonetheless Wrong way to sneeze. Here, a hand, tissue dangling loosely, blocks the viciously expelled contents of nose and mouth. This blockage may be effective in the short term, but it is desperately hazardous in the long range. Soon, that sprayed-upon appendage will touch objects, which, in turn, will transfer their germs to all who touch them. If you must sneeze the Wrong way, wash your hands to minimize spread of germs.

Figure 2 depicts a convenient and chaste alternative to the grimy Into-Hand Sneeze. It is the Into-Elbow Sneeze. The technique is simple: Lean toward either arm, lodge the nose and mouth into the crook, and sneeze away. Though perhaps less elegant, not only will you avoid spreading saliva and mucus, you won't even have to search for a tissue.

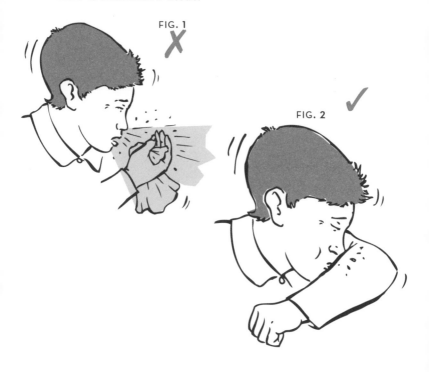

FIG. 1

FIG. 2

Blow a Bubble with Bubblegum

Expert advice from Kelsey Lea, America's 2004 Dubble Bubble National Bubble Blowing Contest Champion, and winner of international "blow-off" against the U.K. Dubble Bubble Champion

A well-shaped pink and glossy bubble of gum is a thing of beauty. Such art requires a mastery that is sadly lacking in many a young girl and boy, struggling to scrape the sticky, rubbery remains of failure from their cheeks and eyelashes. Such a public humiliation is, of course, the result of a definitive lack of attention to the rules and conventions of blowing a bubblegum bubble.

The Wrong Way to blow a bubble is to rush the gum, to smack it impatiently against your teeth for little more than a few minutes before huffing and puffing your burgeoning bubble into oblivion (see Fig. 1).

The Right Way requires patience. Ensure you have the tools: Enough gum and enough time. You will need three pieces and 15 to 20 minutes to chew all of the sugar out. When every trace of sweetness has been

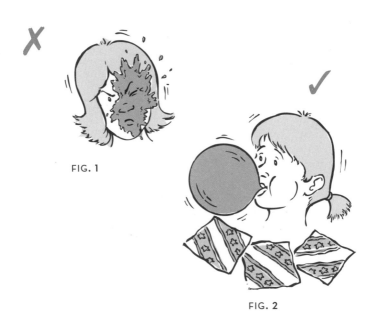

FIG. 1

FIG. 2

purged from the wad, wrap it around your tongue. Carefully and steadily blow through your mouth. Exhaling or inhaling through the nose will cut off the flow of air to your bubble and diminish its size. When you are satisfied with its proportions, or when your lungs are empty and the skin of your bubble dangerously taut, use your tongue to block the opening at the base of the gum and trap the air inside (see Fig. 2). Pause to savor the simple elegance of your creation.

Squeeze a Tube of Toothpaste

Expert advice from Christopher White, member of
the Tube Council of North America

"Squeeze from the bottom and flatten as you go up."
Repeat this mantra to all in your household who are so
quick to forget. How quickly, carelessly some unscrew a
cap and portion out dentifrice from a toothpaste tube's
center. This method is troublesome. It is the Wrong Way.

FIG. 1

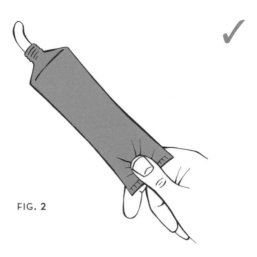

FIG. 2

Toothpaste tubes—most commonly made of laminate—are pliable, but not springy, easy to form, but difficult to re-form. Squeeze from the center or top of the tube, and you will wind up with both an excess of paste trapped below the compression point and paste cascading out and an unsightly, wrinkled tube (see Fig. 1). Extricating embedded paste from the bottom of an improperly squeezed tube is a thankless task.

Instead, squeeze from the creased end of the tube, and enjoy a neat, continuous flow of refreshing paste—with a minimum of waste (see Fig. 2). Guests to your bathroom will thank you, too: A well-squeezed tube is nearly as gratifying to behold as it is to use.

Open a Bottle of Champagne

Expert advice from Philippe Boucheron, wine journalist
and author of *The Independent Traveller's Guide to
Champagne: The Region and its Wine*

Provided your bubbly is properly chilled to between 40–45°F (4–7°C), provided you plan to pour this liquid pleasure into tall, tulip-shaped flutes, and provided your champers is the real deal (not some non-French, sparkling imitator), then—and only then—are you ready to pop the cork.

The Right Way to open a bottle of Champagne requires a paradigm shift. One must think of the task not as removing the cork from the bottle, but as removing the bottle from the cork. Keep this concept in the forefront of your mind, and you are halfway to your bubble-powered buzz.

Remove the foil on the bottleneck to reveal a metal crown and cage. Keep the top of the bottle away from you and station your non-dominant thumb over the crown and cork. Use your dominant hand to loosen the wire cage completely—no need, however, to pull it off. Maintain pressure around the cage and cork, keeping the bottle slightly elevated, and slowly turn the bottle—not the cork (see Fig. 1). The cork and bottle

FIG. 1

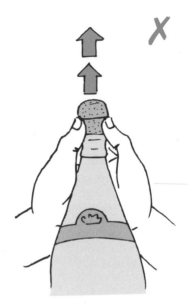

FIG. 2

should separate unhurriedly, as two lovers loath to part. A nice, quiet release of gas will indicate the final separation—the liftoff, as it were.

The Wrong Way, of course, is to shake the bottle or to push the cork out with your thumbs (see Fig. 2), causing the wine to flow out the top of the bottle, imitating a fountain. It might look nifty, but it over-aerates—and, quite frankly, wastes—the libation.

Get out of a Car

Expert advice from Diana Mather, co-founder of The Finishing Academy, Cheshire, U.K., and author of *Image Works for Men* and *Image Works for Women*

Underwear is a very private thing—like religion. One assumes that the person standing next to them is wearing a pair and one is happy to make that assumption on faith, without a personal experience. But on occasion, the presence of underwear (or lack thereof) is proven to the acolyte, and the revelation of this mystery is often due to the Wrong Way of disembarking a vehicle.

The Wrong Way to exit a car is to let it all hang out (see Fig. 2). A splayed blundering from the door, legs akimbo, exposing oneself to all and sundry—it is worse if one is wearing a skirt or dress but singularly unattractive even with the presence of pants. In fact, in the skirted scenario, the presence of knickers is a kind of salvation from the Commando.

FIG. 1

The Right Way is infinitely more befitting to the woman within. When the car comes to a halt, wait for the door to be opened for you from the outside (or failing that, do it yourself while you are seated and facing forward). Press your knees and ankles together and swing them smoothly to arrive at a 90-degree angle from the front of the car (see Fig. 1). Place both

X

FIG. 2

feet on the ground, take hold of the door with your closest hand and gracefully stand, pushing off from the seat with your other hand and using the door for support.

Maintain your mystery, ladies, whether you are wearing knickers or not.

Pose for a Camera

Expert advice from Tamela Edwards, anchor for
ABC's *Action News*, Philadelphia

Nature produces very few supermodels per year. The rest of us—we, the majority—would be wise (and more attractively portrayed) to heed a few simple do's and don'ts when facing the unforgiving lens of a camera.

Do: Set yourself at a slight angle for a soft profile.

Don't: Face the camera straight on, as in a mug shot.

Do: Sit erect, with loose shoulders.

Don't: Stiffen up or slouch.

Do: Relax and think happy thoughts that travel to your eyes (see Fig. 1).

Don't: Pull a face that will embarrass you and destroy your memories in the future (see Fig. 2).

FIG. 1

FIG. 2

Remove an Adhesive Bandage

Expert advice from Nancy Musco, R.N., Manager of Product Education
for Johnson & Johnson Consumer Companies, Inc.,
makers of Band-Aid® brand bandages

Popular opinion says that the best way to remove a sticking plaster or adhesive bandage or tape is to yank the thing off in one swift stroke. Popular opinion is wrong. The "best" way is in fact the Wrong Way. Ripping a bandage off quickly doesn't just hurt, it also strips the top layer of skin and disrupts the healing process by disturbing—or even detaching a portion of—the lesion (see Fig. 1).

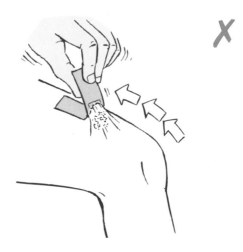

FIG. 1

The Right Way to extricate a stuck-on strip is to approach the object from both ends simultaneously, going from outside in, thereby avoiding unnecessary pulling on the wound. Use fingers to hold down the skin under the tape's long edges as you gently peel away the plaster (see Fig. 2). Think of it this way: You are pulling the skin away from the sticking plaster rather than the plaster away from the skin. You are also assuring your wound will continue to heal—and minimizing additional pain for an already painful region.

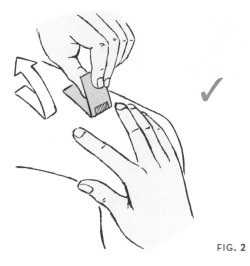

FIG. 2

Tie a Shoelace

Expert advice from Ian Fieggen, Australia's foremost shoelace authority and founder of www.shoe-lacing.com

Another trauma of childhood to be avoided as one grows older is self-inflicted scabby knees from tripping over the loose and flapping untied laces of the leather lace-ups or practical runners worn to school, day in, day out. The secret to a secure shoelace is not the style of knot. It's the knotting style.

The Wrong Way is a volatile, twisty mess of unevenness, as indicated by telltale lopsided loops (see Fig. 1).

FIG. 1

FIG. 2

The Right Way, where the loops jut perpendicularly and evenly from the center knot is symmetrical, balanced, gravity-resistant, and therefore secure.

Are your loops lopsided, your knot unstable? Never fear, there is an easy solution. Simply reverse your first tying action. If you've been crossing right over left, then tie left over right. If you've been crossing left over right, then tie right over left.

Understanding why this works is not the point here. The point, dear readers, is to avoid tripping over untied laces.

Light a Fire

Expert advice from Don Philpott, an avid backpacker and wildlife
photographer, and author of *The Trailside Cookbook*

Since we're not living in the Dark Ages, make sure you have matches or a lighter—preferably in a waterproof bag—before you even begin.

For a fire that catches with the first match and continues to burn, select a protected site—wind could cause a fledgling fire to blow out or burn out too quickly—and clear some land around your potential fire to prevent it spreading.

FIG. 1

Tinder, kindling, and fuel are all important. The tinder—dry grass and leaves, small twigs, or strips of newspaper—will flare up easily when ignited (See Fig. 1). Slowly add larger twigs, and then the logs. Add them one at a time to ensure the fire has enough oxygen to sustain combustion and to make your fuel supply last longer.

Singeing a log in an attempt to show that you can make fire as well as any prehistoric man isn't going to cook your steak (see Fig. 2). And never light a fire if a strong wind is blowing or when under cover, such as in your tent.

FIG. 2

Start a Mexican Wave

Expert advice from Illes Farkas, Eötvös Loránd University, Hungary,
co-author of article in scientific journal *Nature*, discussing
the key conditions for Mexican Waves

A failed Mexican Wave is a sad circumstance indeed. It's like speaking to a stranger when you have food lodged between your front teeth—socially uncomfortable for all parties involved.

Well-executed waves, however, are a testament to the efficacy of group effort. As they rise and fall, circling through a stadium, they seem to say: We are human! We can work together!

The trick here is timing: A wave's success is secured by the ability of participants to stand up and to sit down. Therefore, the action must be initiated only when spectators are seated—not, as illustrated in Figure 1, when some are already standing.

FIG. 1

X

It is also important to begin the wave during an optimistic lull. To start the wave when the home team is losing, when the score is tied, or when the audience is otherwise engrossed in play is a doomed approach. If the crowd is not with you, you're guaranteeing your wave will never crest.

The best waves occur during a stoppage in the action, a time when the audience is enthusiastic but not otherwise entertained: In soccer games, for example, during the halftime break, or, in baseball, between innings. Don't go it alone, either. One must recruit those seated near you. An optimal number is 25 to 35 spectators.

Starting from one end of a bank of seats, stand, raise your arms in the air, and sit (see Fig. 2). These three actions should take no more than one second. By the time you are seated, your nearest neighbors should be standing, creating a rolling effect.

Shouting "olé" as you stand is optional, but is, arguably, much more fun.

FIG. 2

Blow out a Candle

Expert advice from David Constable, holder of the Royal Warrant
as Candlemaker to the Prince of Wales

Admittedly, the best way to extinguish a candle's flame is via snuffer. In the absence a snuffer, one must rely upon the lungs and lips. One must, in the words of Lauren Bacall's character in *To Have or to Have Not*, "Pucker your lips and blow."

The key to putting out a candle orally is moderation and a dry mouth. Blow too strongly, and incommodiously displace the molten pool around the wick, onto the table or the cake. Blow too wetly, and have other odd splotches to clean up or eat around (see Fig. 1). Blow too weakly, and be forced to blow again. A moderate, well-directed wind—mastered only through practice and commonsense (see Fig. 1)—will not, thank goodness, set the world on fire.

FIG. 1

FIG. 2

The blowing out of birthday candles rates almost as an Intermediate Level Skill. Luckily, lung capacity increases with age. Besides, avoiding a light wetting of the cake and the necessary removal of splatters of wax from the icing are all part of the fun.

INTERMEDIATE LEVEL

- ✓ Shake Hands
- ✓ Make a Bed
- ✓ Pack a Suitcase
- ✓ Put on a Pair of Pantyhose
- ✓ Shave
- ✓ Lean in for a Kiss
- ✓ Mow the Lawn
- ✓ Dry out an Umbrella
- ✓ Sit at a Desk
- ✓ Eat a Cherry Tomato
- ✓ Wrap a Gift
- ✓ Fold a Shirt
- ✓ Make a Cup of Tea
- ✓ Hold a Baby
- ✓ Leave a Party
- ✓ Ride an Escalator

Shake Hands

Expert advice from Marjorie Brody, Certified Speaking Professional (C.S.P.),
Certified Management Consultant (C.M.C.), and
Professional Certified Coach (P.C.C.), Philadelphia

Forget winning friends and influencing people: A person will get nowhere in life if he or she demonstrates an inability to execute a proper handshake. Shake hands the Right Way, and make meaningful contact. Shake hands the Wrong Way, and you may as well raise that hand into the air and wave farewell.

Note the handshake offered in Figure 1, with hand hanging limp, lethargic, uncharged, and generally

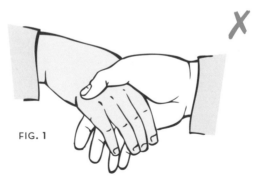

FIG. 1

FIG. 2

worthless. This flaccid palm-to-fingers posture may be suitable for female royals, but for the rest of us, it's inexcusably wimpish and downright wrong. Not that the total opposite—a tense, muscular clutch that presses and paws and clenches like a vice—is any better.

A savvy hand shaker has a confident, moderate grip, as displayed in Figure 2. Outstretched, energized, gripping resolutely, prepared to meet flesh with flesh in one meaningful but modest shake, ready to participate in humanity's highest form of body language. Now that's a fair shake.

Make a Bed

Expert advice from Josie Sauzier, Executive Housekeeper,
The Ritz, London, U.K.

Sheets, pillows, quilts, underlays, and bed partners all combine to provide one of two things each evening: a good night's sleep or a bad night's sleep. A good night's sleep in a wrinkle-free, warm, cozy bed results in a good day ahead. A bad night's sleep fighting over the sheets and blankets and waking up at 3 A.M. on the floor makes for bags under the eyes and broken relationships.

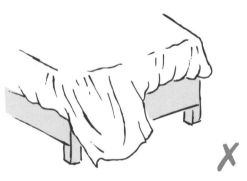

FIG. 1

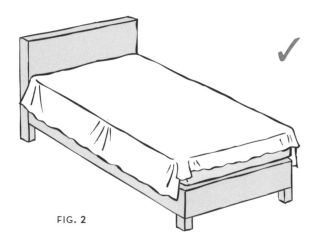

FIG. 2

The key is to ensure that the bottom sheet hangs neatly and symmetrically before you start. Cover the entire mattress with an equal amount of overhang on each side and at each end (see Fig. 2).

Say it: hospital corners. There are two ways to tuck in a bed sheet for maximum comfort and smoothness of sheet. There is the tight, neat, germ-free, hospital-corners method—the Right Way (see Fig. 3)—and there is the slapdash, gather-and-stuff method—the Wrong Way (see Fig. 1).

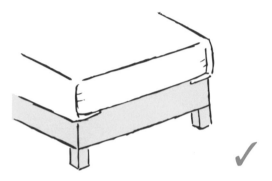

FIG. 3

Equality and neatness might not be things that first spring to mind when you are considering the top ten things you want from your bed, but they have the power to bring about virtual household utopia.

The hospital corner, tucked in at the bottom of the bed, firmly anchors an equal amount of covering for both bed occupants, and only the most vigorous of sleepers will be able to wrench the sheet from both corners to hog it for themselves.

Pack a Suitcase

Expert advice from Genevieve S. Brown, Editor of
IndependentTraveler.com and freelance travel writer, New York City

Packing a suitcase is an exacting science—a strategic exercise in maximizing space and minimizing wrinkles.

Under-packing your case is as wrong as over-packing it. Under-pack, and even the most carefully laid clothes will shift and crease while your luggage is in transit. Over-pack, and not only will you be unable to close your suitcase (see Fig. 1), but you will also look like a bag lady when you don your creased and crumpled clothes on arrival at your destination.

The Right Way to pack a suitcase begins with deciding what to take and ends with not taking too much. "Travel light" should be your new mantra. Lay out what you want to take on your bed and and plan some outfits. Then cut what you want to take in half—you can wear some things more than once.

FIG. 1

There are many schools of thought to which one can subscribe for the actual pack. Advocates of the Interlocking Method propose folding pants, long skirts, and dresses around other items of clothing to prevent creases (see Fig. 2). If you are traveling with a duffel bag, which is too unstructured for this method, pack a rolled T-shirt at the pant fold to prevent creases. Maximize space in a case or duffel by rolling cotton T-shirts and stashing socks and underwear in and around shoes, and in other nooks and crannies.

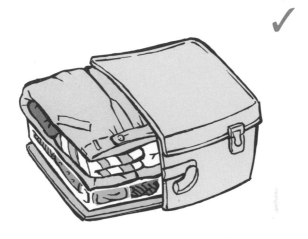

FIG. 2

Delicate items—blouses, shorter skirts, and scarves—should be packed at the top of the case, where they won't be crushed. Pack odd-shaped items in the center of your bag, surrounded by non-delicate clothing.

And an advanced tip: Always take toiletries and makeup in a carry-on bag. Spills ruin clothes and the last thing you need is to spend time trying to clean sunscreen off your clothes when you should be applying it to your skin on the beach.

Put on a Pair of Pantyhose

Expert advice from Forums Administrator
for Stockingshq.com

The wearer of hosiery must take great care during the initial phase of dress. It is at this time, when the stockings/pantyhose/tights/what-have-you voyage from their place in the dresser to their place upon the legs, that these garments are at the highest risk of incurring unsightly blemishes in the form of snags, pulls, or—the most dreaded fate of all—runs or ladders. Practice proper techniques in hosiery donning, and your most delicate of garments will enjoy a long, silky life.

There are two schools of thought about the Right Way to put on a pair of hose. One school says it suffices to have manicured hands (see Fig. 1) and pedicured toes. The other, more cautious, school insists that only hosiery gloves will do. Both schools agree that bodily surfaces must be as perfectly smooth as possible. They also agree on a general technique: Ruche each leg of the hosiery to its toe before sliding one foot in, then the next, alternating sides, cautiously elevating the garment to its desired level (see Fig. 2).

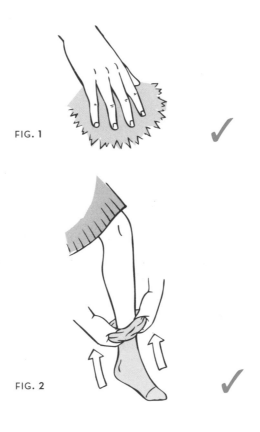

FIG. 1

FIG. 2

Both schools of thought also agree on the Wrong Way to put on a pair of pantyhose. This is to pull on the legs of the hose roughly, simultaneously, and hastily (see Fig. 3), as if they were made of something other than fine silk (or more often nylon). Use this method and suffer the consequences: Your leg coverage will be blown.

FIG. 3

Shave

Expert advice from Eric Kraus, Vice President of External Relations, The Gillette Company, U.S.A.

A red rash across a strong, masculine jawline doesn't send girls weak at the knees. Neither does the opportunity of acquiring such a rash oneself have image-conscious women throwing themselves at the ruggedly, scratchily unshaven. A good shave is essential man maintenance, key to attracting or holding onto your special someone.

Water is the key to a good shave. The Right Way to soften wiry facial stubble is to bathe or shower beforehand. If an all-over cleansing is not an option, then a two-minute application of a warm, wet cloth against the skin will do nicely. Ideally, this wetting should be followed by a hydrating shaving product, available in gel or cream forms. Next, a sharp razor should gently follow the direction of the hair's growth, making sure not to miss errant follicles (see Fig. 1). Rinse, pat dry, and, if feeling particularly inspired, moisturize.

FIG. 1

The application of aftershave has healthy properties. The alcohol in it—apart from stinging—braces the skin to close the pores, preventing ingrown hairs. The scent is just a bonus, really. However, remember that too much aftershave is not a good thing. While it might cover up other less-than-hygenic smells, suffocation is something not sought after on the morning commute.

FIG. 2

The Wrong Way to shave is, simply, to do so on a dry face. A dull razor won't cut it, and while there is a school of thought that advocates shaving against the grain for a smoother result, this process will end in more nicks and the employment of toilet paper for an unscripted role. But go without water, and not only will you miss out on a close shave, you might as well rub your face with sandpaper.

Lean in for a Kiss

Expert advice from Jennifer Worick, U.S. dating columnist,
Match.com, and author of *The Worst-Case Scenario Survival Handbook:
Dating and Sex*

Is there really any need to explain the importance of kissing properly? We all know that the flames of passion have been fanned—and world's shattered—from a single lip-locking encounter. Yes, there is a Right Way to kiss. And yes, there are infinitely more Wrong Ways to do so.

Figure 1 lays out the basic steps of made-in-heaven kiss execution. Two faces must be within striking distance—

FIG. 1

less than an arm's length—of each another. Moving slowly but confidently toward one another, the heads gently tilt in opposite directions, effectively avoiding an awkward bumping of noses. To ensure safety and to convey singlemindedness of purpose, eyes remain open until the point of lip—not tooth—contact, at which time they close. (The rest is up to you.)

Figure 2 shows how not to kiss. There are countless ways to ruin this romantic process and all possibilities cannot fit onto the page. Moving in too quickly, tilting heads in the same direction, closing one's eyes, and baring teeth are among the many feasible pitfalls. The best means of avoiding them: diligent practice.

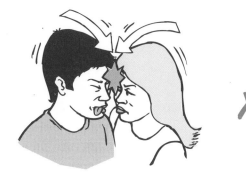

FIG. 2

Mow the Lawn

Expert advice from Bill Klutho, Manager of Public Relations,
John Deere Commercial and Consumer Division, Maryland

If a man's home is his castle, then his lawn must be the well-appointed grounds. Lacking the funds to employ a suitable groundskeeper, the task of keeping the green plot presentable falls to the king.

Lawns should be mowed when they are dry. It is also better to cut too often than not often enough, particularly if you want your grounds neat and tidy, rather than sporting something akin to an unattractive lopsided hairstyle. However, it is widely agreed that the key to lasting, lush, and neatly tailored grass is variation of mowing course.

The Wrong Way to mow: plowing straight into a knee-high field of grass (see Fig. 1). Not only will you destroy your mower, you'll be lucky to have a lawn after chopping it off almost to its roots.

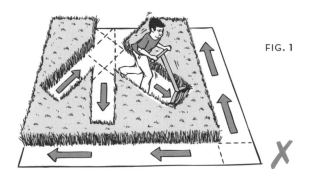

FIG. 1

The Right Way to mow: Start off by mowing the perimeter of the lawn. Work back and forth across the lawn in strips. Orient yourself to a straight line and overlap the strips slightly. Mow like this and you'll create stripes in your lawn that would make a greenskeeper jealous. Be sure, however, to vary the direction you mow the next time round. You don't want to get in a rut—literally.

FIG. 2

Dry out an Umbrella

Expert advice from Jonathon Wardle,
James Smith & Sons Umbrellas, U.K., family business founded in 1830
and reputed home of the London umbrella

The sheltering action of the umbrella is something that is taken for granted until it is noticed to be lacking.

Umbrella care can be summed up in one statement: Keep it dry. But obviously not when it is raining. Return the favor that your umbrella graces you with, and the two of you will enjoy a long relationship.

The first step to drying the umbrella the Right Way is to get rid of excess water when stepping inside after a downpour. Hold the closed—but not rolled-up—umbrella by its handle. Firmly but gently tap or jab the umbrella to shake the droplets loose. Also hold the ribs—the metal bits that poke out on the edge of the canvas—while tapping or jabbing (see Fig. 1). Once the excess water has been removed, simply open the umbrella and leave it on its side somewhere safe (see Fig. 3).

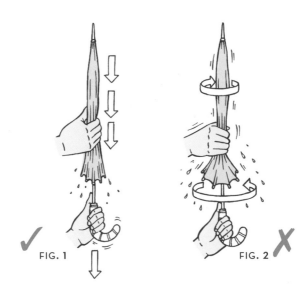

FIG. 1   FIG. 2

Never, ever dry out an umbrella by twisting it. The umbrella ribs are not built for this motion (see Fig. 2). Twisting puts a great deal of stress on them and brings you a lot closer to a broken umbrella.

Do not roll up an umbrella before it is fully dry. The water can rust the umbrella or mold can grow on the canvas.

The Wrong Way to set an umbrella out to dry would not be damaging to the umbrella so much as it would be to the next user. If you leave an umbrella upside-

FIG. 3

down so that the dome shape is inverted to a bowl shape, water will pool up at the bottom and drip over the next person to pick it up.

An advanced tip: If you are out and about when it stops raining and are not able to dry your umbrella properly, close it but do not roll it up. This will keep the umbrella aired until it can be dried out the Right Way at home.

Sit at a Desk

Expert advice from Tina Worthy, Registered Ergonomist,
Ergonomics Society, U.K.

Sitting sedately could be a dangerous pastime. It is something you do every day and probably for a large proportion of it. But sitting at your desk is not straightforward. Science has gotten involved and eager ergonomists—as odd as their branch of science might sound when spoken out loud—maintain that sitting at your desk the Wrong Way can lead to serious back and neck strain, and general discomfort.

Good posture is an essential skill that must be employed when you sit at a desk. Figure 1 shows someone sitting the Right Way. Note that she is sitting up straight, with relaxed, "open" joints, and her body (or x-axis) angled at a little more than 90 degrees from the floor (or y-axis) with elbows, hips, and knees angled at approximately 90 degrees. The backrest of the chair is adjusted so that it supports her lower back. The

FIG. 1

Right Way equips you with good circulation and a generally good demeanor.

The Wrong Way to sit at a desk (see Fig. 2)—slouching, slumping, or bending forward at the waist in a chair—equips you with discomfort, fatigue, and backache. Sit consistently the Wrong Way and the corresponding postural problems will follow you for life.

Consider the tools of your trade. Is your computer screen directly in front of you at eye level (see Fig. 1)?

FIG. 2

This is the right position, the pain-free position. If your monitor is too low, you will crane your neck forward (see Fig. 2); too high and you'll tilt your head backward, resulting in neck and shoulder pain.

Consider your chair. The correct chair height allows your elbows to hang comfortably at about the same level as your desk and be in line with your keyboard. It is Wrong to sit for too long without a break, you need to move around to keep good circulation and reduce muscle fatigue.

Eat a Cherry Tomato

Expert advice from Cheri Sicard, co-creator and Editor of
www.FabulousFoods.com, California

The deep, red blush of a cherry tomato is always enticing and the ripe aroma of this summer fruit is almost intoxicating. Some maintain that the humble tomato has aphrodisiac powers—the French call them *pommes d'amour*—but it is plain that eating a cherry tomato the Wrong Way will not net you any admirers, let alone lovers.

FIG. 1

Cherry tomatoes are small, slippery little suckers with a potentially explosive payload poised to destroy your shirt. The Wrong Way to eat a cherry tomato results in a shoot-out whose trajectory you cannot predict—and untold damage to unsuspecting clothing (see Fig. 1).

The Right Way treats the tomato with the respect it deserves. If a tomato is offered to you as an hors d'oeuvre, approach it with confident fingers, place carefully in your mouth, and chew with sealed lips, enjoying the sensation in a locked-down environment. If a cherry tomato is presented to you in a salad, to avoid your shirt becoming a combat zone, gently prick the skin of the fruit with your fork before popping it whole in your mouth if it's small, or carefully cutting it in half (see Fig. 2).

FIG. 2

Wrap a Gift

Expert advice from Melanie Nerenberg,
Director of Special Services at Kate's Paperie, New York City

A gift without the wrap is like a cake without icing. It's still good, but it's not quite as good as it could be. Wrap a gift sloppily, with paper bunching this way and that, tape affixed slipshod, bows tenaciously tied, and you may not experience present rejection. You will, however, feel present dejection.

There are two factors to keep in mind when gift-wrapping: space and tools. Seek out a hard, flat, clean surface—no bed, thank you (see Fig. 1). Remove surrounding clutter, including beverages.

FIG. 1

X

FIG. 2

Set your gift wrap—paper is easiest—facedown on the surface. Center the boxed gift—also facedown—on the paper. Fold the paper tightly upward, so the edges meet at the center (or, if you're up for a challenge, so that its edges form a seam at one backside corner).

Inspect thus far. Is there excess paper in any direction? This is the time to shear it away, using a sharp pair of scissors. The first seam tape—double-sided Scotch is best—is the long one, using one, long piece of adhesive. Again, be sure the paper is taut.

The next seams are on the box's edges. Fold in the smallest edge, then the two longer edges, all in the forms of trapezoids or triangles. Affix only the longer edges by folding one over the other. Ribbons are optional.

Fold a Shirt

Expert advice from Cristiano Chiarello, Manager,
Casual Men's Wear, Harrods, London, U.K.

Your appearance speaks volumes about your personal habits. A wrinkled shirt shouts: "I care nothing about how I look. Be happy that I'm clean, buddy." While many women's tops and men's extra-fancy shirts should always be hung, basic collared dress shirts and shirts for casual wear need only proper folding before retiring into a drawer.

The Wrong Way to fold a shirt is to crease it directly down the center. This ensures an unsightly wrinkle every time down the middle of your chest and a wrinkly collar. It may make putting the laundry away faster, but it betrays slovenly habits. It is also entirely wrong to fold an unbuttoned shirt. This is the quickest way to destroy its shape.

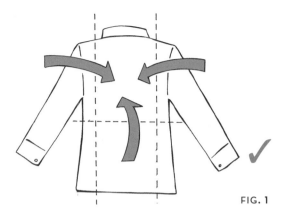

FIG. 1

The Right Way to fold a shirt starts with laying the shirt buttoned-side down on a flat surface (see Fig. 1).

Step 1: Fold each of the sleeves back, so that they meet in the middle.

Step 2: Fold one side of the shirt lengthwise to the midpoint of the back. Repeat on the other side.

Step 3: Fold the bottom upward to the collar, about a third to half of the way up the length.

Step 4: Flip the shirt over to check the collar is intact.

FIG. 2

Your shirt is ready for setting into a drawer and you have entered a new age of wrinkle-free wear (see Fig. 2).

A word of warning: The Right Way swiftly becomes the Wrong Way if you stuff your neatly folded shirt into a crowded drawer or leave it in a pile (see Fig. 3).

FIG. 3

THE RIGHT WAY TO

Make a Cup of Tea

Expert advice from William Gorman, Executive Chairman,
United Kingdom Tea Council

Few things are more disappointing than a badly brewed cup of tea. Whether you are presented with a watery concoction, under-infused, or a stewed solution, unfit for consumption, this humble beverage has the power to divide work colleagues and families alike.

To make a perfect brew, you must first start with good-quality tea—loose-leaf or bagged, either is acceptable—that has been stored in an airtight container at room temperature. And the key: Boil the kettle with fresh water each time you want a cuppa. The best flavor is extracted from the tea leaves when the water contains oxygen (see Fig. 2)—the oxygen levels of the water reduce each time the water is re-boiled.

To ensure a strong enough solution, allow for one tea bag or one rounded teaspoon of loose-leaf tea for each

FIG. 1

cup to be served. And don't forget to steep the tea for the recommended time before dispensing it into your drinking vessel. Pour the tea or remove the bag immediately and you have a weak, insipid drink—you may as well heat up dishwashing water. Leave the bag or the leaves in the water too long and suffer a bitter brew.

FIG. 2

And a note on adding milk: The Right Way to make a the perfect cuppa in a mug with a tea bag is to make the tea first and add the milk second. This ensures that the scalding water concentrates on the tea bag and is not diverted in heating up the milk. The Wrong Way is to dump cold milk onto a tea bag and then add the boiling water (see Fig. 1).

Hold a Baby

Expert advice from Dr. Cheryl Hausman, Primary Care Physician, Children's Hospital of Philadelphia

When accepting a newborn into your arms, think head first. Babies less than two months old lack neck muscles developed enough to keep their noggins upright. It would be wrong to hold a wee one straight up and down, because his wee head would topple to his wee side.

If this happens to you—or, rather, your baby—fret not. The baby won't break. But he may bawl (see Fig. 1).

X

FIG. 1

FIG. 2

The Right Way to tote an infant (see Fig. 2):

Adult: Arms bent into a cradle position, palms of hands facing up.

Baby: Stretched out and also facing up; back of the skull nestled into the crook of one adult elbow; tiny bum and itty-bitty toesies stretching down toward the adult wrist and up the adult's other forearm.

Alternatively, you (the adult) may handle him (the baby) by holding the little one's body in one hand and the head in the other.

Leave a Party

Expert advice from Joanne Adcock, U.K.-based freelance Events Manager, who has organized parties at a range of high-profile events, including the 2006 Winter Olympics and the MTV Europe Music Awards

Departing a gathering the Wrong Way can leave a bad taste in society's mouth. Leaving a gathering the Right Way, however, leads to sweet social success.

The trick to painless party departure: brevity. Note how the partygoer in Figure 1 has entangled himself in the crowd, pausing to bid adieu to every

FIG. 1

Tom, Dick, and wife-of-Harry whom he's encountered during the evening.

Our partygoer in Figure 2 knows that one need not make verbal acknowledgment of the evening's every exchange. A polite nod to anyone who catches his eye will do.

The only person this guest must valiantly seek out: the host, to whom he briefly offers sincere thanks. If the host if nowhere to be found? The invitee would do well to conserve precious time—and write a thank-you note the following day.

FIG. 2

Ride an Escalator

Expert advice from Jason Collins, Manager of Waterloo Station, London Underground's station with the most escalators

Too many escalator riders are unschooled in the mores of moving-stairway navigation.

Figure 1 demonstrates a mobile stair in peril. Escalator Passengers A and B unwisely stand two-abreast, stanching the transit of Escalator Passenger C. Note Escalator Passenger D, imprudently roosting at stair's end, a hazardous blockade to A and B. All wrong behavior.

Figure 2 shows Passengers A through D in good form. Escalator Passengers A and B graciously perch to the right, still able to carry on their conversation, while assuring smooth on-the-left transit by the hurried Escalator Passenger C. Escalator Passenger D, in her turn, displays thoughtful placement: She fixes herself at the side of the stair's end, far from danger and near to the hearts of her fellow passengers.

FIG. 1

FIG. 2

ADVANCED LEVEL

- ✓ Enter a Hammock
- ✓ Hold Chopsticks
- ✓ Smoke a Cigar
- ✓ Make an Entrance
- ✓ Greet Royalty
- ✓ Pack the Trunk of a Car
- ✓ Carve a Turkey
- ✓ Tie a Bow Tie
- ✓ Dance the Tango
- ✓ Parallel-Park
- ✓ Hit a Golf Ball

Enter a Hammock

Expert advice from J.R. Pelletier, Director, The Hammock Company,
Greenville, North Carolina

A hammock is proof that careful, concentrated effort can reap pleasant reward—and that a careless approach results in an unhappy ending. Board this slung *chaise longe* the Wrong Way, and suffer an injury to your pride (and your bottom) when you tumble to the ground. Ease in the Right Way, and luxuriate in a most embracing repose.

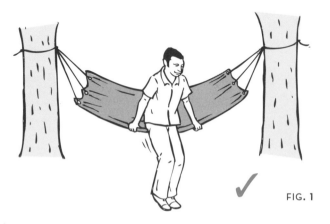

FIG. 1

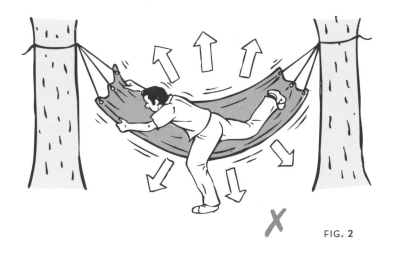

FIG. 2

Propriety of position and deliberateness of movement are the keys to successful hammock entry. Observe Figure 2, illustrating the perilous crawl-in approach, a method that further destabilizes the naturally unsteady swing. Note how this hammock appears as if it might flip the crawler onto his back. It will.

The Right Way is infinitely less hazardous. Standing with his back at the hammock's midpoint, the entrant places his hands to the sides of his body, pulling the hammock's center closer to his posterior (see Fig. 1). He sits down—slowly, now!—easing his backside into the belly of the hammock, and then carefully rotates 90 degrees to bring his head and feet to opposite ends of the recliner (see Fig. 3).

FIG. 3

Hold Chopsticks

Expert advice from Susanna Foo, owner and head chef,
Susanna Foo Chinese Cuisine, Philadelphia

Have you ever found yourself whispering to the waiter at an Asian restaurant if you could please have a fork? Don't waste your time glaring at the neatly packaged pair of chopsticks lying next to your rice; learn how to use them as an expert would.

The key to maneuvering a pair of chopsticks adeptly is to keep your fingers relaxed as you remember that one

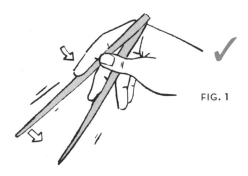

FIG. 1

stick remains stationary and the other moves to grasp the food.

First: Hold one chopstick—pointy side down, of course, as you would a pencil—resting on your middle finger and grasped by your thumb and forefinger.

Second: Slide the other stick into your hand so that the thicker part is resting at the base of your thumb and the thinner part is held steady against your middle and ring fingers.

By bending and unbending your forefinger and middle finger you will be able to pivot the top chopstick effectively to pick up food (see Fig. 1). Don't hold the chopsticks too close to the pointy end; it's much easier to hold them about one third of the way down from the top.

The Wrong Way to use chopsticks has a lot more to do with rudeness than ability to eat. Being clumsy with chopsticks is excusable. Being impolite with them is not.

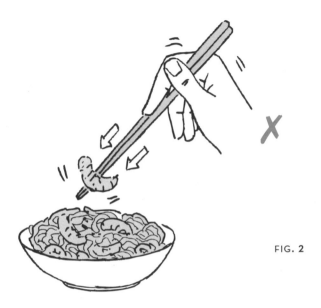

FIG. 2

Never wave your chopsticks about or point at people with them. Do not spear your food with the chopstick as if you were a caveman catching a fish with a rudimentary weapon (see Fig. 2). And most of all, do not lick your chopsticks. Not only is it offensive, it could be painful if you end up with a splinter.

Smoke a Cigar

Expert advice from Oded Ben-Arie,
Mike's Cigars, Bay Harbor, Florida

Cigar smoking is fraught with protocol that extends before and after the actual smoking. A cigar must be stored correctly (uncut, and in a humidor). It must be fresh (not dried out; it must remain silent when gently squeezed or rolled). Its cap must be cut cleanly (not pierced), sliced at its shoulder, about one eighth of an inch from the tip—and no deeper—preferably with a miniature guillotine (see Fig. 1). It must be warmed

FIG. 1 ✓

FIG. 2 ✗

FIG. 3

with a torch or wooden match—but never a smelly benzene lighter (see Fig. 2)—before being lit in the traditional way. Pass the end through the flame during a few even puffs until the entire circular tip glows completely red. With these criteria met, the smoker may proceed.

The Wrong Way to smoke it: Inhale quickly and deeply. Do so, and feel dizzy to ill from the cigar's high acid content. Instead, smoke it slowly—the Right Way—and carefully, so that the tip remains evenly lit, taking approximately one shallow puff into the mouth, not the lungs, per minute (see Fig. 3). Finally, when finished, gently place the remaining tobacco into the ashtray so that it will extinguish itself.

Make an Entrance

Expert advice from Natalie Glebova, Miss Universe 2005 and consultant for *Universal Beauty: The Miss Universe Guide to Beauty*

There are many Wrong Ways to make an entrance at a party or other social event. You could poke your head inside the doorway. You could walk in, fumbling with the contents of your pockets. You could enter looking down, looking away, or looking angry (see Fig. 1). These wrong actions would not prevent you from entering the room. They would, however, prevent others from minding as you enter the room, not taking heed of your obviously heed-worthy presence.

Essentially, these wrong actions cause an entrance not to be made. (It goes without saying that the inverse is true: Make too grand an entrance by blowing kisses and performing a beauty-pageant wave, and expect to be written off as a pure hack.)

The Right Way to make an entrance causes the persons in the room to notice you without noticing they're noticing. It makes these folks aware that you are there and that there is something about you that is attractive beyond your natural attractiveness. Making an entrance is a nuanced undertaking. Luckily, there is a Right Way to do it.

Step 1: Accomplish all those petty tasks before crossing the threshold. If there is a cloak to be removed, remove it; a business card to be procured, procure it; a stray hair to be arranged, arrange it; a nose to be blown, blow it.

Step 2: Stand up, straight and tall. Inhale deeply. Think: Grace, confidence, elegance. Step through the doorway purposefully. You are not hurried or harried. Nor are you are dazed and snail-like. You are poised. You are approachable. You are confident. Look at you! You are smiling. (But not too much.) Observe Figure 2.

FIG. 1

Enter. And—here's the trick—pause, just for a second, to make sweeping, wordless, and ever-so-brief eye contact with the occupants of the room. Think to yourself: "Hello! Nice to see you! I am so happy to be here!"

FIG. 2

Dally not in the doorway. Move on and in. Extend a hand to shake, if appropriate. Nod the head, if the occasion so calls. Or just pronounce a simple greeting— "Wassup?" will do—to you new admirers.

Greet Royalty

Expert advice from Rick Fink, English butler with
forty-five years' experience serving in stately homes, and teacher
at the Butler-ValetSchool.co.uk

There are no obligatory codes of behavior when meeting and greeting a member of a royal family, and formality has been relaxed to some extent, but there is definitely a Right Way and a Wrong Way to greet a Royal.

The Right Way is also known as the Traditional Way. Many people meeting their betters wish to observe the traditional forms of royal protocol. For men, incline the head, bowing from the neck only. A deep bow is no longer necessary. For women, perform a small curtsy (see Fig. 1). Others may prefer to shake hands in the usual way. (For the Right Way to Shake Hands, see page 50.) It is protocol to wait until the Royal extends his or her hand first, however.

On presentation to a king or queen, the correct formal address is "Your Majesty," and "Sir" or "Ma'am" for

FIG. 1

subsequent address in further conversation. For those not ruling from the throne, the formal address is "Your Royal Highness" for first address and subsequently "Sir" or "Ma'am."

The Wrong Way to greet royalty finds its roots in Over-familiarity or Lack of Respect of their position and station. Close personal interaction is not encouraged and touching is a definite thing to avoid (see Fig. 2). Even a light touch on the back. So, hands off the

Queen! It is also wrong to show your back to a Royal—
this is considered disrespectful—to shake hands with
gloves on, and to leave a room in which a Royal is
present before they quit it.

A few things of note. While these rules might stand you
in good stead in many Western countries, do not
assume the Right Way to greet European royalty is the
Right Way to greet Asian royalty. And if you are not a
citizen of the kingdom over which the Royal rules,
you are not required to curtsy or bow, just treat them
with respect.

FIG. 2

Pack the Trunk of a Car

Expert advice from Mark Sedenquist,
Editor of RoadTripAmerica.com

Before we enter the realm of how to fit what in where, a word of advice: Check the level of air in the spare tire first. That is, check it if the tire resides beneath the floor of your trunk, and you're about to pack that trunk with luggage. It seems like good sense—and it's quite simple to do—but few of us actually do it. This type of neglect is wrong—and feels even more wrong when a flat tire coincides with a full trunk.

Common belief says a certain type of person—even a certain gender of person—is the best installer of humankind's many goods and chattels. This is not true. Packing a trunk requires no expert. It merely calls for commonsense planning and compartmentalization.

Begin with a clear vessel. A messy trunk with useful but random items stashed in it does not make for easy access (see Fig. 1). In summer, store ice scrapers in the garage. In winter, pack away the beach gear. Keep all safety equipment—jumper cables, reserve fluids, flashlights, flares—in one, easy-to-reach banker's box. Reserve accessible trunk real estate for this box. Do not cover it. Plan to pack around it. It would be wrong—and a shame—if an emergency arose and you needed to dig through your vacation wardrobe in order to find the first-aid kit.

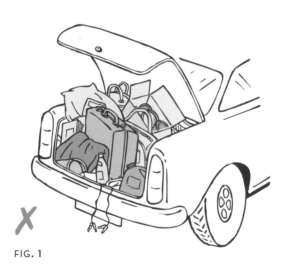

FIG. 1

The rest of the unclaimed terrain is yours to settle. Working back to front, insert largest items first, sliding them to the farthest reaches of the frontier. Next, add medium-sized bags. Last, the smallest (see Fig. 2). All the while, be sure that overnight bags and kiddie treats are packed close to the front, so that when the children cry out for a new DVD/old teddy/fresh snacks, you need only to pull over, pop the trunk, and, with no muss or fuss, snatch and deliver the object of their desire. Such are the joys of a rightly packed trunk.

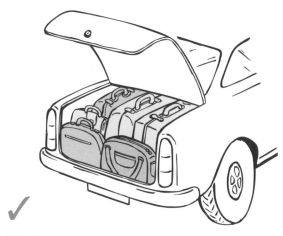

FIG. 2

Carve a Turkey

Expert advice from Sam Martin,
author of *How to Mow the Lawn* and *How to Keep House*

Carving a holiday bird requires a sharp knife, a little know-how, and a fair bit of courage. Not only do you have to stand at the head of the table delicately slicing the evening meal into palatable portions, you also have to look good doing it, while avoiding a mistimed

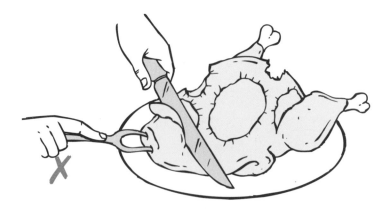

FIG. 1

downward stroke that could send the turkey flying across the room.

The Right Way is about the all-important first cut. Miss the first cut opportunity and you open the bird (and yourself) up to indelicate presentation of hacked and chunked meat that mixes white and dark meat and adds to the stress and bickering over the family meal (see Fig. 1).

Step 1: Stand at the head of the table with the platter turned so that the bird's legs are pointing to your right.

Step 2: Using a fork to steady the beast, cut down between the leg and the breast, finding the thigh joint. Cut off the leg and thigh through the joint. Repeat for the other leg. On a separate plate, cut the leg from the thigh.

Step 3: Now, cut off the wings. Slice down between the wing and the breast, finding the joint.

Step 4: Carve the breast, slicing from the outside toward the breastbone in long, thin pieces (see Fig. 2). Then turn the platter and repeat from the other side.

It's a good idea always to wear an apron. You'll need something to wipe your hands on every so often. And no matter how neat and careful you think you are, if you are carving, you'll splatter your clothes, covering yourself in your meal before you've even sat down at your place.

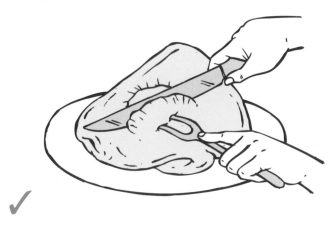

FIG. 2

Tie a Bow Tie

Expert advice from Kirk Edward Hinckley,
founder of bowtieclub.com

Part of the magic or mystique about wearing a bow tie is the aura of difficulty in tying one. It is actually quite simple, using the same knot as when one ties one's shoelaces. Impressing fellow wearers of formal wear is not hard as long as the Right Way to fasten a bow tie is well-practiced.

Step 1: Pull your collar up and out of the way. Dangle your untied bow tie around your neck, with the longer end extending about an inch and a half lower than the shorter end (see Fig. 1).

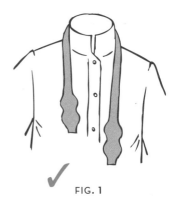

FIG. 1

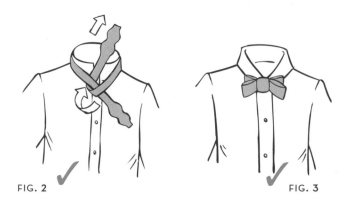

FIG. 2   FIG. 3

Step 2: Keeping in mind that the longer end should work around the passive shorter end, tie the two ends in your most basic wrap-around knot.

Step 3: Fold the shorter end into the hourglass shape of a bow and hold it horizontally against your neck (see Fig. 2).

Step 4: Bring the longer end over the middle of the bow.

Step 5: Form the longer end into an hourglass shape as well, and pull it under and behind the bow made with the shorter end.

Finally, fold down your collar neatly.

After it is secured it may be uneven or a bit messy. Feel free to adjust it, but don't fuss with it too much. A slightly off-centered look will remind everyone you tied it yourself, plus women find it almost irresistible to come and straighten that slightly imperfect bow.

It is all too easy to tie a bow tie the Wrong Way. Being a stickler for a too-perfect knot or ending up looking like a badly wrapped gift (see Fig. 4)—in instances like this, it is best to call up the trusty clip-on from the bench. There is no shame.

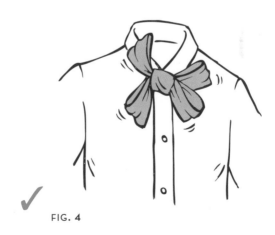

FIG. 4

Dance the Tango

Expert advice from Mauricio Castro, founder of tangodiscovery.com
and renowned dancer and teacher of Argentine tango

There is more to the tango than thrusting a rose into your mouth and commandeering a dance floor. It is a dance of leadership and submission, a sexy strut, its style and stance connecting two people emotionally as well as physically.

A poor tango partnership belies a lack of chemistry between the dance duo. Distance from your partner, a reluctance to dance cheek to cheek, flat feet, and lack of commitment to the stance—droopy arms, in particular —make for an artless dance (see Fig. 1). And modern feminism has no place here. The man leads this dance, no exceptions. Of course he should not drag his partner around the floor, but should firmly and steadily be directing the movements of the dance. Equally his partner should be responsive to his movements, not in a rush to anticipate, or attempt to

FIG. 1

take the lead. The tango is the dance of a couple, not two mismatched individuals.

To tango the Right Way, imagine that you are a great jungle cat. The smooth fluidity of movement, the stealthy step performed on the balls of the feet—not the tiptoes—produces the perfect posture for this dance (see Fig. 2). You will know the right posture as it will give your body pleasure—if it feels good, it is sure to look good.

FIG. 2

Arm position is also very important. Your arms should be straight and steady. However, while a firm and steady hold on your partner is desirable for dancing in unison, a vice-like grip that slowly crushes their bones and dancing spirit is not.

And watch the traffic. The dance floor is likely to be filled with couples dancing in unpredictable directions. Being continually interrupted by bumps and crashes is not the Right Way to perform the tango. Keeping a vigilant watch for rogue couples is essential.

Parallel-Park

Expert advice from David Toms, Driving instructor,
UK Driving Instructors Confederation

The thought of parallel parking on a busy street can induce a paralyzing fear. The effects of this fear can mean city gridlock as one drives forward and backward, feverishly trying to slot the car into the space, or lengthy journeys, as one circles the streets looking for a space to enter nose first. Face your fears and never drive 20 miles to go and get milk again.

The Right Way is a conscientious and confident adherence to a set of simple steps that will have you safely off the street in no time. Observe Figure 1. Pull up next to the car in front of the clear space, parallel to it at a distance of about 2 feet (0.5 m). Make sure you have your indicator on and check your blindspot, to make sure the way is clear.

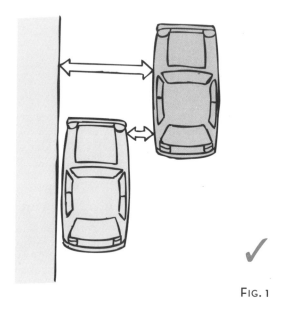

FIG. 1

Put the car into reverse and back up slowly. Now is the time to invoke the mantra: "Slow car, fast hands." When the back of your car is level with the end of the parked car, turn the wheel until the car is positioned almost 45 degrees from the curb (see Fig. 2), then straighten the wheel.

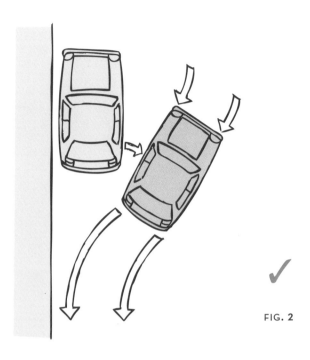

FIG. 2

When the back of your car's front door is in line with the rear bumper of the car beside you, and the back of the car is approximately 1 foot (0.25 m) away from the curb, steer rapidly to the right. Slowly back into the space. Your car should be 6–8 inches (15–20 cm) away from the curb when you are parked.

The Wrong Way to parallel-park is simply a neglectful approach to the task. They may be called "bumper bars" but parking should not resemble a fairground dodgem ride, nudging and bashing your way into a space (see Fig. 3).

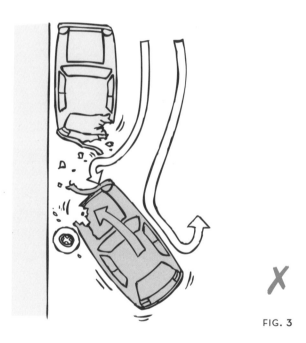

FIG. 3

Hit a Golf Ball

Expert advice from Robert Cotter, Director of Instruction at InstantGolfLesson.com, and former golf ball design engineer

Hitting a golf ball can be easy (even for the least athletic among us), but hitting the ball where you want it to go takes a lot of practice. It all begins with proper positioning and the right swing.

It sounds simple, yet it is surprisingly easy to miss when swinging at a completely stationary ball. And that is not even mentioning the skill necessary to have the struck ball follow the intended trajectory through the air.

Imagine that your body is the hub of a bicycle wheel and your arms and club are merely an extension of the hub (like the bicycle spoke). In the golf swing, your body (the hub) generates the power as it coils and uncoils back and through, and transfers this power to the arms and club. The ball merely gets in the way of the clubface at impact and is sent on its way.

FIG. 1   FIG. 2

The Setup: Imagine you are standing on a railroad track. The ball sits on one rail, and you stand on the other with your feet, hips, and shoulders parallel to the rail (see Fig. 1). Your feet should be spread to about the width of your shoulders. The grip should be secure but soft, about a 3, on a scale of 1–10.

The Backswing: Move the head of the club straight back along the imaginary ball rail for about 45 cm (18

FIG. 3

in), and then as your body rotates, the club will rise to the top of the backswing (see Fig. 2). The club should be almost parallel to the ground and your hands will be opposite your right ear. The butt end of the club shaft should point along your imaginary ball rail line.

The Downswing: Now for the fun part. Start the downswing by bumping your hips towards the target and rotating your body (the hub) all the way until you face the target (see Fig. 3). This causes a chain reaction as the body unwinds sending the power down your arms, through the shaft to the clubface, and then into the ball. Remember to have soft arms so they can respond to the uncoiling of the body. Call out "Fore" as is necessary.

It sounds easy, but many people instinctively snap the club up with their hands and arms in the backswing and then incorrectly use their arms and hands in the downswing. Manipulating your hands isn't necessary. It actually decelerates the club (which is bad), and the leading edge of the clubface will start moving up (which is also bad). All the hands and wrists have to do is hold on.

Don't rush your swing, or grip too firmly or loosely (remember the 3-out-of-10 pressure). This will help you avoid the ensuing embarrassment of sending your club flying rather than the ball (see Fig. 4).

X

FIG. 4

Index